TRUTH & OTHER ABORTIONS

Tony Tackling

TRUTH & OTHER ABORTIONS

Tony Tackling

ISBN 978-0-9570850-6-0

Published by Wivenbooks 2013
www.wivenhoebooks.com
Book design by Catherine Dodds @ Jardine Press

All rights reserved. No part of this publication may be reproduced, stored, or introduced into a retrieval system, or transmitted, in any form or by any means, electronic, mechanical, photocopying, recording or otherwise, without prior permission of the author.

Cover illustration: Richard Storer, 2003

*for Sophie,
because they were*

Contents

vi. Preface by Dr. Paul Elliott

1

3. A light stops from the estate through the window
4. A Question
5. The Waiting Room
6. In Spirit
7. Poetry Cue
8. Run to me, I can barely stand
9. After Lowell
10. out of the Rose
11. La Pasionaria
12. a night collapses
13. Li Po
14. The Dolphins
15. Seventy-eight
16. Old Heath

2

21. Because you're worth it
22. Mirror
23. One from Many
24. Ramsgate
25. The Flood
26. Nelson
27. Early May
28. A Sun
29. In a second hand bookshop
30. music/blood
31. Foreground: Jars of Spirit
32. Cycle
35. Death at the turn-in to Haynes Park
36. Good night, Haven Road

3

41. Long Wyre Street
42. Heathrow Flight Path
43. the scene
44. Circular Road
45. The House on Greenstead Road
46. By the route
47. Last Poem of the Year
48. past playing
49. From the café
50. Tsang-kie
51. Thought for Food
56. New Cult
57. Wivenhoe Park

4

61. I will not die on Maudlyn Road
62. From Colchis
63. a dream of the Top Bar
64. After it All
65. Distance
66. Night, Summer
67. poem
68. Sculpture
69. The General
70. Ardleigh Green Road
71. Promise
72. Wivenhoe Revisited
73. Truth & Other Abortions

Preface

I first read Vladimir Mayakovsky's *Talking With the Taxman About Poetry* in the mid-1980s when it seemed as if poetry might be able to present itself, once again, as a revolutionary force. Little did we know at the time that the danger to poetry would not come from the constricting power of Right wing censorship but from the diluting effects of neo-Liberalism and global communication. The internet is awash with poetry now; it's everywhere, on blogs, vlogs, in on-line journals, on websites and in databases. If we could tax all of this we could end world poverty for all eternity.

A new book of poetry then is something to be treasured, not only because it has been worked on, changed, thought over, and revised but because it is now part of the physical world, your physical world. This book is now your responsibility.

Poetry is perhaps the hardest of all art forms because we are all born poets. However it is also an art that we continually strive to forget, that we attempt to grow out of. This is why, for most people, poems tend to make their appearance in moments of drunkenness, love-sickness or grief, creeping up on us when we are not looking. This is perhaps the reason why we experience the familiar pang of embarrassment when we find the poems we have written years later. "I was not thinking straight" we say, and file them away with the photographs of ex-partners and old recipes.

For some however poetry is more than this momentary itch; it is a way of viewing the world, a perspective. They have their share of drunkenness, love-sickness and grief too but this is only the first stage in a long process of creation that results, at the end of it, in a poem. It is this willingness to work that distinguishes the poet from the rest of us.

This book is written by such a poet, someone who never stopped believing in the worthiness of the creative act. It is uncompromising in its dedication to a tradition of poetry that strives for universality and permanence against the forces of homogenisation and transient fashion. On a personal level this collection reminds me of the University of Essex poetry readings where some of them were first recited. I remember it always seemed to be raining, or at least windy and cold, and some of this has certainly found its way into the poems themselves; they are songs and odes to minor tragedies, alienations and disappointments that, like all good writing, encourage us to suffer them, shrug, then move on.

These poems are saturated with place (the endless rooms, the windows, the parks, the streets) and are indelibly marked with those who have influenced them (Li Po, Pound, Eliot, Williams, friends, girlfriends). However they are also a testament to the difficulty of producing poetry and a reminder of its necessity. They are the work of a flaneur, an outsider looking in, but they also remind us that good poetry is only ever about two things: the eternal nature of the everyday and the everyday nature of eternity.

Dr. Paul Elliott

1

A light stops from the estate through the window

A light stops from the estate through the window,
things make sense;
out in the car park an alarm goes off,
quickly quieted.

There is light early when the clocks go forward,
though you've less time to sleep before a job that kills all this,
the gathering beauty.

Sometimes I don't know what to say to you
as you try to get some rest.

Pour a drink,
listen to great music,
try writing
poetry.

A Question

There was a brass band by
    the lake.

'What the fuck's that?'

'What?'

'Out there. There's a brass band by
    the lake.'

They stood still,
in black military uniforms;
it looked like a navy funeral.

'I can't see.'

'By the fucking lake. Jesus.
It's like a navy funeral
or something.'

'I can't see,' she said,
without trying.

He watched, buttoning his shirt.
Then he sat down on the corner of her
mattress and pulled on his boots.

'What're they doing out there?'
he asked himself.

He pulled on his jacket and
left her flat.

The Waiting Room

He died when he was sixteen.
The tumour was diagnosed when he was
thirteen. He could play
every Buddy Holly song when he was eleven,
on a red Stratocaster.
And he could sketch anything he wanted.
I'm sitting in the surgery besides
a sketch of his he donated,
a sketch of a sailing boat, sails down,
docked at high tide.
The pencil work blurs slightly
around the curving hull of the boat
as if the slight ripple of waves
and the boat are one.
It's dated from '94, the year before he died.
He's been dead fifteen years.
In the centre of the waiting room is a
box of toys, old toys, ones I remember
from my youth. Orange spacemen
in grey spaceships, yellow skittles,
orange hoops. A young girl with
red hair is rummaging through them;
occasionally she lifts something to show her mother
who's sitting across from me reading a magazine.
I turn back to the picture. His name
is sunk in white on a black plaque
beneath it. 'Tony Tockling', the receptionist
calls over the speaker, though she is only
a few feet away, and I stand up, stretch
and walk down the corridor to his office
where he asks me where the pain is.

In Spirit

All have seen you arrive, gliding,
your bronze feet swift
beneath an ankle length white dress, floating
to a seat at a table, far.
One watches as you depart.

Poetry Cue

The table is full of yellows,
when I am red.
But I'm tired of green.
Outside is black with rain.

Run to me, I can barely stand

By the Hythe,
even the dead tyres in the mud mean movement,
and the deflated football screams into the top corner.
The stars are unhealthy on the green water.
I see my love in the distance through a traffic fog
and I cry she must run to me,
I can barely stand.
Flowers are plastic and painted silver in the local florist.
The road works are empty through the night,
for all the holes we dig ourselves.
It's been raining, but the rain has stopped briefly
and I let my hood down
and walk through the puddles I see,
it's less effort.
The bottoms of my trousers are wet and heavy,
but they will dry shortly,
after I am sat down inside,
and the world becomes the view from a window
mixed with bourbon and romance,
and the crucial air of untruth.

After Lowell

I am the New Englander;
religion grows gently from me
weak, over-watered;
a true New Englander.

Robert, your serious form
creeps towards mirage,
like elephants;
a slow troupe of family.

Past years
have been long and so
softly too has the sun
dried all cries.

The stairs, after this poem,
will not creak, from love,
and the hard space next
to you, filled.

out of the Rose

      the gulls float
          white lines above the quay
coming down
      breeze carried to the straight green
              water. they settle,
    fluff their wings
   float again and then
            take again to the breeze
circling
   looping
      playing
           to an audience.
              I join them
  with this beer and pen
        playing to an audience
and all is man-made
        this early March warmth and brightness
     and damn it all
         I have no child
    nor
        want

La Pasionaria

Did you wander Vizcaya?
I heard, with a tray bore
of sardines on the head?
And Catholic?
Woman dressed in black,

before the miner from Asturias,
and your children,
and prison? You wait
to stand—Shut up Sotelo!
We know your aims!

Eyes ringed in black,
bruised with sorrow—
taken a beating from
fate—but strength,
dignity in contemplation—

Lies,
these lies make me wretch.
You hold a cold knowing gaze—
determination. You stand,
the Cortes quiets—

A voice fills this place,
but not song, nor
scream—it's simple, direct,
no rhetoric, theatrics—
It is a constant force.

My comrades wonder—
they propagate—
where come your words?
The East?
De un corazón que sufre…

I am no priest, Dolores,
but you take my uncollared throat
between your words—
you paint your grave lips
red with me.

a night collapses

the eyes of my pussy grow cold,
grow cold, and question
clumsy words, nervous
insults. There are never enough cigarettes
when my pussy is cold,
I've never enough places
to leave for.

Li Po

Ah, moon looks huggable in wine river
rippling red and there is not the sadness,
joy! in a jade boat bottle.
It is in the delicate vines, white with tinted gold,
gracing image of your place and time,
and the myth of embracing your name,
I choose with a fine, midday rioja.

When I was king's son
a spit twirled day long and corks flew and women,
gilded by all tones of the orient,
offered their flavours.
We knelt thankful,
floating hands neat before eyes
caught on east-breeze.
I may infer hypnosis, though it lacks the splendour
this world beauty conjures,
as in the slight fingers, painted nails,
we lose all needless,
and that moment least, lasts all ever.

Today, town, your red buildings do not offend as I
slide into the pussy of the moon.

The Dolphins

Her father was snoring so hard it rattled
        the thin walls
        between the bedrooms,
and I listened whilst she slept,
    slept tight in a ball,
        away; it was early summer.

      Between curtains patterned by dolphins
    began
the lightening into paler blue of the sky
    and the song of birds,
    the hum of a milk-float.

      I gently left her
bed and began to dress.
      There was too much to begin
to lay with her.

A carpet softened exit
    from the sleeping house
    brought another new street,
       morning.
    And across, a neighbour
getting into his car to leave
    for an early shift;

      a noise heard often, that
      peeling car.

In the rapidly advancing sun,
    the windows of her house became torches,
       so bright
    they left temporary scars
      on the retina—
the open window on the second floor right,
    more than any—

whilst the dolphins floated outwards,
    away on the curtains,
      appearing to swim
on the mid-dawn breeze.

Seventy-eight

I got on the bus,
with only a five pound note
late for a meeting
and the driver said, no change.

I had waited too long
and began to say
when an old man I'd never known
asked what I needed, son.

eighty p.
here.
thank you.
he waved me away.

I sat at the back,
watching his thinning hair
and hands atop his stick
waving with the bus.

at my stop,
I thanked him again
and he said
you're welcome, son.

Old Heath

We started walking one Sunday
and didn't stop.
We walked onto a military base with warning signs
and didn't stop.
There was a hidden lake behind dead trees
and massive tyres
filled with empty cans.
There was always another path leading to another field,
we didn't stop.
The sun was out in January
but it was cold.
Nothing was all right.
We were broke and worrying about money.

2

Because you're worth it

Kerry was popular,
she rolled her skirts up,
she wore higher heels than most of the other girls
and dark lipstick.
And like out of an American teen cliché
she dated the captain of the football team.
Then at a sleep-over
her friends found shit stains in her knickers
and her life was destroyed for the next few years of school.
She even stooped so low
as to hang around with us,
never saying a word.
Once after a P.E. lesson
an old friend of hers threw a used tampon at her
which stuck to her forehead,
and it became policy
for the in-crowd
to sneak turds into her bag whenever they got the chance.
My friends and the rest of the boys in our year
watched all this happen,
not just with Kerry,
but with every girl in school.
They never stopped fighting with one another,
friends becoming enemies,
vicious rumours,
blackmail, jealousy,
bullying of the worst kind.
All the male bullies ever did was beat you up,
the girls took the hearts and the minds.
My group of friends lasted from year one through to the end,
no group of girl friends ever lasted more than a term.
I've never understood the expression:
'If women were in charge there'd be no wars'.
Perhaps it was just true of a time long gone,
      but now,
maybe it's 'Maybelline',
or the 'Hollyoaks' omnibus…

Mirror

You see and hear
as though we are mirrors
you hear and see

I understand and to some
degree
sympathise, yet

your thoughts

interest me
more than I interest
me, like me

you don't know
why. Why don't you
know?

One from Many

Something about looking down
on a path beneath a street lamp
which figures.

He falls over drunk
and his head bounces
but there is the movement,

strength
of the drunk,
he gets back

up.
He begins again to walk
again, from side to

side.
It's alright, he'll
wake tomorrow

with a bruise and a
cut. A scene from
a movie

has happened,
his movie,
from this tenth floor.

It's twenty to two
and elsewhere the wind is
still and warm.

Ramsgate

The sons tilted the armchair
                where he'd sat
listening to local radio,
    very low,
with the television on mute,
and padded the thin plastic weaving
              for anything left.

In another room
        the still-wrapped palette
from a grandson's French trip
brought silence.
        A model gladiator's helmet
found behind the bookcase and a book on
                ghosts.

In the garage there was a face,
    Jesus,
a crown of thorns ringed about the forehead,
        eyes opened wider than any,
        mouth was tightly shut,
        neck messily severed,
a hand pulled the hair up.

        And a picture of
a daughter in-law
        which was kept.

The seagulls wailed as the dirt was cleaned from the windows.
The green moss on the roof tiles.
        And between the rooms, hard wooden borders
jutted from the dark patterned carpets,
        seen for one last time.

            There was an echo of a warning:
    not to run,
        not to fall.

The Flood

A Greek from the fish & chip shop
runs into the traffic, scooping down
for the clipped pigeon. The clipped pigeon panics.
It circles puddles; rain
floods our street, the drains are stuffed;
the sky is white, the air is white,
the goddamned world is white,
and this is an English summer.
Through flooded street the traffic slows.
They wait for each other to pass where the water is deepest.
Then hope arrives in a council van
and a man gets out, as the drivers sigh
before they see him stick down a triangle with red borders
       that just reads 'flood'.
Then he gets back in the van and drives off.
The Greek walks with the bird
around the back of the flats
and sticks it in a cage I've never seen before.

Nelson

The dog's got a big gash on his side,
where they cut out the cancer,

how curled he sleeps without that collar
that plastic cone round his neck.

he's in his basket
and I'm writing a poem

and both of us are alive in the light
and both of us have left behind thought.

Early May

Another sky is white;
the clouds spread themselves,
a thin line of pale blue
in the distance.
It's almost as though
Summer bides its time.
A note is hit, the bass,
before the chord is flicked
and the room before the window
is filled.

A Sun

I saw a house surrounded by walls, and I wanted
to sleep in the fields surrounding it. I wanted
to pass the mass of days away in neither. And I wanted
the rebirth of passion to begin in either.

For what when people come to disturb
armed with news of darkness in London,
of drowning in the red sea – pilgrims –
AK-47 democracies, but still,

is it best for a profile shot, or back?
To close my ears and only to music open
them; the company is weak on the ground
floor; I am stronger in the upper shade.

An island, far from Greenland,
and a woman with a piano and grand sonatas.

In a second hand bookshop

Ah, this morning I was sweeping outside,
sweeping away the dead leaves and such,
for which I normally use a bag
—I sweep the dirt into a bag—
well, I'd neglected to bring one out with me,
so I left my neat pile of dirt and leaves to be scattered
....by the wind—
yes, a bright morning,
....but quite a breeze on her—
I passed a small car parked across the road
and noticed a woman at the wheel,
seeming to hunch forward rather sharpish,
and a lad in the passenger seat,
I wouldn't be surprised if it was her son,
resplendent in baseball cap,
sank into his seat, half-turning away,
which I thought peculiar—
(He drew out 'peculiar' into the mouthpiece)
—I thought maybe they were watching me.
Well, these days one can never be sure.
I left with a copy of Williams.

music/blood

(it is the music
that catches us

    unbalanced;

        yr. second caught;
like hanging dead
eaten,
    in a room you beat in…..

between heart and lungs are
percussion—strings
coming through teeth/chiming
mind
    xylophone/abstract

the poem is a tuning fork
meet the tune with every player—

        symphony, O!

Foreground: Jars of Spirit
from a picture of Grandad painting

He's scraping the white from an oriental dress,
bowing towards the woman,
eyes bruised with concern.
She's turned her back.
Both the hand and the drive are mine.

Cycle

I
the lever has been born
deaf and quixotic
still born but it's vague
and warm

the vital signs are knickers
on a horse
flickering by electric
heat

glass grope from
tobacco desk, forlorn
the rest
is the source

from which dim joint
a torn
man in a wrong frame
cogitates

vegetates
goes towards
weird reflections
on perfume necks

II
he grinned at me,
dusting himself off
and said he was okay
I noticed with dismay
his grimy penis
out of fly
weeping like a cry
when a loved one dies
when your insides' dead

I asked if he was fine
I could tell he was on wine
from the bottles in the gutter
I could tell it didn't matter

III
and we're supposed to fix the pieces together
to make a whole that makes sense when we know
nothing makes sense and there is no
goodness, thanks

IV
the dogs are beautiful; big, healthy
and full of spit
they are like miniature horses and role about in mud
and love us

huh, that's good
I'm glad you've found a love like that
I bet they shit whole mountains
and piss rivers

V
in the rectory today
I saw a priest
who took my 20p and blessed
me

I saw the stains
on the glass
and the sun coming through
them

what is that
I said
to nobody
nobody said

what it was
but I saw
people coming
apart

it was enough
to will me outside
into the grey hound
and chase

VI
a brilliant grey, black
a red so wonderful
hell, it's brick
and a sky so moist
so white
dance from that Shenfield train
with steps unburdened by sex,
by identity
into Romford.

then die
as you come
to understand
the long black smudge
cross the life canvas
a portrait of me before
being no Mona Lisa I
cannot deny him
his truth

Death at the turn-in to Haynes Park

A guitar, tuned, ready, sunburst.
An eleven-year-old boy in the back.
    Traffic eases forward,
        past the evening.
There is a whirling of lights up ahead,
    blue lights whirling.
When they come they see
legs and feet, still,
    beneath a red car, still,
and they are late.
And all the late traffic
    eases forward
        past the evening.

Good night, Haven Road

He walks along
the street beneath
our window,
from dark to bright
in the night
beneath the street lights.
He is normal,
except his left arm jumps around,
the wrist loose,
it flails and waves
and does not die;
it swings and dips and revolts.
And the cars come past
in stereo to me,
sweeping into the distance.
His face glows
as the headlights approach;
he stares into them
until his face is obscured
by darkness,
before the next light.
Naked,
I turn from the window
and wake up Sophie
and take her to bed.

3

Long Wyre Street

He was my tramp
until I quit my job.
I would buy the magazine
give more than the cover charge
and never read it.
I gave more than the cover charge
because he could use the money more than me.
Also, the first time,
I stood there waiting for change
with him staring at me
before I realised I was being somehow impolite.
Then I quit my job.
Sophie became the one who bought the magazine
and he stopped even looking at me.
He was no longer my tramp.
I'd walk past him alone and broke
and have to say, sorry, no thanks.
He stood at a crossroads
so there was no avoiding him.
When I was still working
I walked past him once
and we exchanged pleasantries.
He asked me how I was.
I started telling about how much I hated work
before realising what I was saying.
He looked sad,
so I bought his magazine.
He didn't hand it over.
Do you mind?
he asked,
it's my last copy.
If you take it the police will move me on.
What could I say?
Nothing.
I went home
to make dinner
and stare at the ceiling.

Heathrow Flight Path

                                    there is feeling
                                    romance even
                                as the light blinks
                              in the half world of darkness
                               casually ascending
                               a diagonal path
                               up in the night
                              and it doesn't matter
                             destination doesn't matter
                           it just feels good
                        romantic
                   some of us are going somewhere
                 are near the moon
               can see London
             a chaotic fury of lights
           like ants on fire
         put whiskey with ice
       and a blank page before
     and keep it there

the scene

the scene

played until night
        my
            self

andyouyourself

played on alone
        our
            space

became wide, night
betrayed my

wish, and all this
destroyed this

Circular Road

The full summer, camouflage green,
trees and fields, brown wooden fencing,
golden horses,
circling, like petals, my love.

The House on Greenstead Road

It stood out, a house in a road otherwise
naked and brick red, age grey;
a long road of close, identical, terraced housing;
lives piled on lives, families on families.

It stood out, coated in strong greens, overgrown
bushes, trees, tumbling messily
onto the pavement. You wouldn't notice
unless you'd walked past a hundred times,

but it lived there. How often do you
study such uniform housing on your way
to work? Private, different, the door only
visible for a moment, through an arch of weeds.

It would've been easy to conclude
the house deserted, left to become alive
with the mould of the soil, but for the car parked
out front, a disabled driver sticker in the window.

It made me ready for work, that house did,
the secrets it held, the refreshing darkness,
that brief glimpse of a door covered with web
with an arch of stained glass window above it:
"home" before red, green and yellow murky coloured fragments of glass.

One day the car was not there, workmen
were busy cutting their way through the jungle,
light was hitting the house for the first time
in decades, perhaps. It was clear in a week,

and after two, I forgot which house it was;
they'd changed the door, there were new windows
a satellite dish had grown from the bricks like a wart,
the wall had been knocked through for a drive.

Soon after, I handed in my notice and moved.

By the route

The swing moves gently in the reflection of the moon,
like a ghost on the pond,
      fading between water and air.
Night has an invisible child,
twisting the chains,
      creaking them over its silence.

Last Poem of the Year

I
London. Hammersmith Rd. Wind coming forward,
rain coming forward, big drops of rain on the wind
moving forward into our faces,
lost. A two-ninety-nine pop up map of grey London, large
green Hyde Park splodge around which streets build, web-like,
but not our streets.
She doesn't mind. She grins in the face of wasted cares,
the rain, the red buses, traffic and people.
I do my best to shelter her match.
We move on and into.

II
The cab driver was screwing us, I
knew the price,
he'd brought it two quid forward, we
were no nearer rest,
talking too much, unaware.
"Anywhere here…ANYWHERE HERE".
It took the last of the money and there was a walk.
It was a night building, winds picking up, in uppercut,
leaves, wrappers, even the rain,
coming up from the pavement.

past playing

    The last wires out,

rusted with young blood
                        by the bridge
whilst a crack in the nut
              means the low E slips.

From the café
for C. Decker

across the road,
through crawling traffic
and pissing rain,
a young boy

stamps and kicks
a deep puddle
at passers-by—
the little bastard.

an older boy,
disinterested, with
one eye on him,
stands near—

perhaps his brother?
his other scans
the jam of cars
as though for a lift

Tsang-kie

Early clusters, bird
feet,

left in the fluvial sands;
we note

progress, or at least
move-

ment—the tracks end
in flight

"They say…that some thousand years before Trojans founded Rome
a scholar named Tsang-kie was commanded by his emperor
to invent Writing…"
Hugh Kenner, The Pound Era, (Faber & Faber: London, 1975), p. 14

Thought for Food

a)
Bus comes down road, rattling
it's night and empty, driver

                         driver, you
                         have to reach
                         station
                         walk

          all these things
          happen / to all these
          things / happening

                how it is put

                rather empty?

this is a positional
a positional
no more about the road with its lamps
       and its rain

                Yesterday the police wait
                in Ayloffs Walk
                information of a riot

                out the college

                        (No, put simply
                        a statement of case
                        tune to a return,
                strip a reality

z)
To my dearest, May-ree,
there are options

        constantly the traffic is force

        force to slow, even, beside Haynes park /

        swamp – rain on dark green leaves

        and a dark green / smell

        not unpleasant,

        gross / womb close

        as in, and beginning of

        grossness

    fucking roads, fucking rain(

      the lighting of a match
      thinking, and holding it to
      an empty mouth
      taking in deep the sulphur
      the flame bends to the lip
      like a fool
      burning

            follow

            the recurring patterns about the lip

            of a Venetian palace

            dripping beige stone

            crucifix tears

            and return, with back to the tip of

            and follow

            the recurring icicles as Americans

            bump into you

            and sigh

an even keel of misery
amongst the study of beauty
more examination of beauty

                    (the music
                is indescribable
             its peaks are yours
         and you follow them as though
     rhythm is universe
             and intake is how
                 you peak to follow
                     the indescribable
                         music

                    this is morning

                    the real, secret morning

                    of the becoming

                    and that sun you see all your life

                    is as fierce as these

                    reported final summers

                    and screwdrivers and loud Russians

                    postpone the unreal

                    impact and reprisal

the email is a thing of evil
        at waking / afternoon / sins
            arrive and where's the bag
                phone Stratford station
                    fathers appear as ogres and scream

evolutionary bouts of wonder and confirmation
despair, fear of death
chest pains

                                      the options,,,,,,,,,,,<

z – b) (meeting with things

        It all matters too much
                like being tied to the mast of a sinking

these knives, forks are toys
this fridge is a toy fridge
and the rattling ice is soon to join
the liquid and I
        understand the toys,
are brought up to join, speak to the young,

                we are dead with our toys and objects
       are, we
            try to break, stoves of plastic
        cardboard empty boxes of food and the girls
the young girls with prams and dolls in the prams
                they piss themselves and cry

smiling)if you hang them
                they close their eyes

and some of us are really immeasurably

sad

                        infused / confused

and it becomes escape, their escape, as meeting on other terms
has been

replaced, by those who've built
in stupidity, without cognitive malice

built!

c stage)
to destroy / pull down now

this is response, no replace
of

but a paper on the Massacre in Rwanda
some hope

would be total destruction of reality
and it has become that
well beyond the dousing
of final bridges back

                    the situation

there is little colour
here

I watch from Rayleigh tower
an intellectual who seems to appear

to care

`   some
hope

New Cult

Christ,
I am positioned
for assault.

The enemy
appears each day,
regular.

It eats me up
it shits me out,
it digests.

I am prone,
as are hundreds,
nourishment.

I suggest
a new cult
against the Eye.

To join,
you must destroy
the glasses.

It cannot see
then. It will blind.
The Watcher.

Consumer,
consumed; break
away and,

with new found
awareness, we
escape, to

build. I play the violin,
write poetry,
paint love.

Wivenhoe Park

   The child dances with a picture
      on the field beside the lake,
jigging, her brother wanders up and
    they both jig. Then they chase a duck
      and their mother watches them.
They've nothing to worry about.
    Whatever the picture is, it's been printed
      on a side of A4, and I can only guess
from up in Rayleigh Tower
    what the picture is of. I hope
      it's a picture of Antonio Benedetto Carpano,
    the inventor of vermouth, because
      I'm drinking a fifth Manhattan,
but that's a long bet.
      It's been a long day.
A gull flies again closely past the window
    and the sun sets. Sophie says something
      about making dinner, puts her book down
and leaves the room. The children stop chasing the duck
       and begin jigging again. It's not
    discovery that matters, it's the poem,
      the memory, the cigar cutter,
    and so I now find the point
and go clip on a Havana bought in town.
      By Christ, I'm here, I am here.

4

I will not die on Maudlyn Road

However the rain comes,
a thick, heavy rain
in which you feel yourself drowning,
or thin and sharp, like needles
somehow coming up from the pavement to pierce your cold cheeks,
I will not die on Maudlyn Road.
I watch carefully the lights of the cars and vans and buses
slicing through the evening
turning the invisible turning,
the wheels sounding an impossible crying;
I see idiots stride cross, not thinking;
let the wheels screech, let there be that dull thud
I've heard in so many movies, television programmes, dreams,
     I think.
I will not die on Maudlyn Road
on my way to a job I hate,
with the same petty managers,
the same shallow co-workers who when asked what they're 'into' reply:
'Nothing, really.'
The same uniforms, the same rules, the same low-pay.
This will all break apart,
this instance of reality is vulnerable.
I am, as you read this, being executed between the lion of St. Mark and St. Teodoro
for smoking a cigar in a restaurant after a dinner of mussels in garlic butter.
I promise you:
my body will be buried besides those of Pound and Stravinsky
on San Michele,
a million miles from Maudlyn Road.

From Colchis

It becomes grey flashes

between the cut green fields,
like smoothed hair
      on an audience.

      so many heads

      down, the beaten floor,
stomach it, every
      footprint,

      all still-full skies,
and banks of rain;

      green becoming
Romford grey.
It makes sense slowly:

the thrusts,
the comings and going,
      our art.

a dream of the Top Bar

the bar is flooded with light
I find an ashtray through the over brimming plates of rotting food
every song on the jukebox is my song
his optics are busted
I have more than enough and it is all good
he doesn't mind and enjoys the atmosphere
he is Christ and there, bang,
I have my religion

a girl my friends haven't warned sits down
and doesn't care anyway when I begin to cry
out everyone can die
this is my song
would you like a game?

After it All

After it all, there is nothing there.
The neat pile is senseless.
Shall we say it? Devoid
of importance. This fool's game
is a fool's game. But afterwards
it's death. One can become too involved.

I have a woman,
an intelligent girl who plays the piano,
can paint and is widely read.
I dream of her at train stations
and at birthday parties.
We live together in Palermo and have six children
all orphans. We bring them up
to be fond of living.

As long as I live I will try,
the two are twined,
and I hold a dead man's grip
on the last bars
of wonderful music.
My breath.

Distance

The delicate branches of the
tall lime, dark against
a March sky,
sway gently in its
wet breeze,
as two sparrows perch

some way apart,
with nervous glances
from ground to sky and back
to one another
again.

Night, Summer

Gulls knowing nothing
wrong
        glide slowly down, so
slow, with eyes black
        to that horizon,
in fact, they're out of
        place to minds
stricken by
        departing suns,
fading redness,
fire as if rain,
        as if static,
on the water,
        which is significant,
if not urgent,
when someplace is waiting,
somewhere you must be,
        but barred,
as they settle against tide,

and make no sound
        nor move.

poem

This smashed clear glass
        on grey asphalt
                is, my love,
caught in the lit
        lifeless square,
                is, my love,
aptly shattered,
        and this piece it
                is my love.

Sculpture

The brushes wiped, packed away,
        canvas bagged, half-finished, broken
                landscape taken of wrong vision,
palette dried in this little sun,
        easel folded quietly.

                The hammer has come to my hand
and the marble I
        stands in a yet foreign valley!
                where darkness and light vie

all is beginning to begin again

                with scratched diagrams on stone
mind set in creation and Yes
        what weather comes, comes
            if I lose my sight
I will trust my throw
        and come to know
            the make of marble
what veins spread through like virtues
        or where the cheap stone might crack and splinter
            not worrying
whether grotesques are born from my art.

            It is thunder
as the first fragments fall ground ways;
        it will take all the strength of this world
            to discover
the shape of what I can sculpt
        myself.

The General

Her one leg poked out
beneath a tartan rug,
an eighty-year-old dyed redhead in an NHS wheelchair.
She laughed and coughed and laughed.
I was reading Heat magazine
waiting for a chest x-ray.
Someone handed her a magazine to stop her laughing,
nothing could stop her coughing I guess;
she scanned through the pages at such a pace she might have been a
    computer
uploading data into a memory bank;
then she flicked to the final page and laughed:
"I ain't got me goggles, 'ave I?" she proclaimed to the room,
"all just nonsense to me."
A nurse called out for a "Mrs. Hawkes?"
She laughed again and said it was her.
"Follow me," said the nurse.
"I can't push me fucking self, can I?" she replied with a grin.
They took her into a room, then my name was called,
and it turned out it was nothing.

Ardleigh Green Road

Staring at the coming
pavement, thin
ginger hair twisting
in the wind,
arms in a bomber
jacket pumping, white
trainered feet
swiftly moving before,
glasses flashing
the morning askance,
lips askew like they are drawn
taught by strings, and
locked, locked,
everyday now, restless
for fifteen years.

Promise

calm please
be silent
once

jesus
you demand
more

attention
I will try
love

Wivenhoe Revisited

He stands, mid-April,
    wiping stains from the ship's hull,
        sun striking the river, and marble
shimmers against blue aft.
    Here again, but not stayed
        the same, setting
why I see boats, still
    or starting for ocean,
        guided by tiller, directions beyond
estimation, and due deliverance,
    down, stated,
        down in the old manner,
where reason is esteemed
    meaning is a stalled craft
        and I must stop.

Truth & Other Abortions

It is time to write you
        a first, final, poem of love
                and then quit,
to go separate ways, as you wish
        me to leave
                as is your right.

When I remember the last years
        I remember your kindnesses.
                I am ashamed
I remember your kindness.
        As you say, I frame all
                by myself.
I won't offend you with denial
        of my selfishness.
        I took and never gave.

.

The sun is on the Hythe.
        It labours to produce buildings
                somehow not so ugly
now, as the area with you
        I will always associate
                becomes already memory
as the past forever does,
        tweaking what is bland
                to beauty.

An image of your hands
   holding my hair back
      fills my eyes.

Flying on the bow
   in the pool in Portugal,
      hills in the distance like westerns,
was the little heaven
   you got in the hell
      of me.

Is a poem ever enough
   to tighten syllables
      about magnitude.
I believe
   the poem must stand,
      a salvageable element
in the confusion.
   Only imagination
      blends coherence
from what will be
   now a chapter
      no footnote
on our divergent journeys
   back to birth.

So I finally give you
   something
      of the only worth of me.

II

I know little
        of the asphodel.
                The only flower I pressed
was you.
        I've learned late
some flowers
                withstand the process,
withstand the page,
        can only be caught,
                petals to the sky.
        Photosynthesis
is far as my botany goes
        and every school boy knows
that
        once clipped a rose dies.

        Those days blackened,
a sky with no stars,
        or more apt
                nights above the town
of Colchester,
        where electric light
                robs the mind of stars
and we feel our time in swamp green
        carpets stained and flecked,
                shards of tobacco like the hair

of a life,
        I have wasted
                yours,
gone as the years gather
        speed.
                I regret,
I would like, nothing,
        to become a poem
               that delights
but this is no time
        to shirk truth,
                truth and other abortions—
I regret myself,
        myself, again
                dragging it back to me.
A cycle
        I cannot fall from.

I wouldn't know an asphodel
        if it grew to dwarf my form
                but I have pressed a flower.

III

There is hardly a bomb
        to grieve
                but a politician's promise

means the backdrop
        of the slight perceived.
                I too
proffer limp sentiments
        in lieu of an apology
                for claiming too much
understanding it was due me.

        Edifices crumble
                taking time to rebuild.
I used to see them built stronger
        until age
                suggests other-
wise—things hit a point
        when cells weaken,
                losing the will
to begin again,
        to come to things new,
                as though things are us
in the grand scheme—
        and I am sure there is no such thing—
                but in the grand scheme
everything
        is
                decaying.
but you.

        If I could plant a garden
                I would make it colourful

and the colour
> would suit
>> the vegetables
so pure to eat,
> and there would be an element of shade
>> where one can rest from sun,
and I would call it your future,
> and would be content
>> to pass,
of an evening,
> on the memory of evening,
>> recalling fragrance.

IV

In the peace of a temple,
> stone on stone, I carve,
>> layering as slates
to build this roof
> beneath which I persist
>> to answer the question:
what is the root and where is it found—

> The root is you,
>> it is found in speech.

This is the ease,
> long sought,
>> you bring me now

  in my temple,
         I lay down,
                 no hope or fear,
                         finds me here.
The slight wind
         carries on,
                 curtains of words
spiralling a ghost
         into the drama
                 of what once was
a gothic room,
         empty as future
                 us in light adjoining
rooms
         and untrammelled
                 sleep.

It is no coincidence
         I can continue forever
                 because I am talking of love.
         Because I talk of love
                 I can never stop
thanking you
         and understanding.
Understand
         this process.
                 Forgive the horror
as you might a pet,
         teeth sharper than it knows,

                nipping the feeding
hand.

I am tired but ready
        for the end sighted—
                strength to strength
I will go,
        and love,
                I will go.

V

But for you
        I will crown the poem
                King.
In your absence
        the fields will wilt
                but not go brown—
it would not fit
        for weaknesses are the very reason
                and the very reason
is all—
        in as much as
                a scarecrow
fools the sparrow
        or the town hall clock
                goes always right—
or rather, Queen,

   as in your name
      the poem is.

VI

   The final hurt
is you taking these words
      not in their spirit offered,
and that turning to art,
   to the poem,
      an absurd is made from emotion.
No wrong is righted,
   give some credit
      to the undeserver.
I cannot talk of flowers
   with eloquence
      unless emotion endures.
If technique is the test
   of a man's sincerity
      follow the music—
though out of this attempt
   I wish well of you,
      I say,
farewell.
   My curious love
      will go on.

   When you've cried,

  not often,
      I feel the sorrow
          of the godly for the godless
  and I am
      not proud
         of this,
  for my god is both
      truth and abortion
         as am I.

  The sun is down on the day
      I began to apologise.
         I'm sure
  I will never stop.
      I am sorry
         I will always be
  me.

Lightning Source UK Ltd.
Milton Keynes UK
UKOW031004020613

211628UK00005B/107/P